MY FIRST BOOK ABOUT

CALIFORNIA

by Carole Marsh

This activity book has material which correlates with the California Content Standards. At every opportunity, we have tried to relate information to the History and Social Science, English, Science, Math, Civics, Economics, and Computer Technology CCS directives. For additional information, go to our websites: **www.thecaliforniaexperience.com** or **www.gallopade.com**.

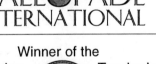
GALLOPADE
INTERNATIONAL

Reading
Reference · Research
Reinforcement

Winner of the
2002 Learning Magazine Teacher's Choice Award

Gallopade is proud to be a member of the National Council for the Social Studies, as well as these educational organizations and associations:

SHOPA MEMBER
School, Home, & Office Products Association

NSSEA

ASCD

The California Experience Series

The California Experience Paperback Book!

My First Pocket Guide to California!

The Big California Reproducible Activity Book

The Coolest California Coloring Book!

My First Book About California!

California "Jography!": A Fun Run Through Our State

California Jeopardy: Answers & Questions About Our State

The California Experience Sticker Pack

The California Experience! Poster/Map

Discover California CD-ROM

California "GEO" Bingo Game

California "HISTO" Bingo Game

A Word...
From the Author

Do you know when I think children should start learning about their very own state? When they're born! After all, even when you're a little baby, this is your state too! This is where you were born. Even if you move away, this will always be your "home state." And if you were not born here, but moved here—this is still your state as long as you live here.

We know people love their country. Most people are very patriotic. We fly the U.S. flag. We go to Fourth of July parades. But most people also love their state. Our state is like a mini-country to us. We care about its places and people and history and flowers and birds.

As a child, we learn about our little corner of the world. Our room. Our home. Our yard. Our street. Our neighborhood. Our town. Even our county.

But very soon, we realize that we are part of a group of neighbor towns that make up our great state! Our newspaper carries stories about our state. The TV news is about happenings in our state. Our state's sports teams are our favorites. We are proud of our state's main tourist attractions.

From a very young age, we are aware that we are a part of our state. This is where our parents pay taxes and vote and where we go to school. BUT, we usually do not get to study about our state until we are in school for a few years!

So, this book is an introduction to our great state. It's just for you right now. Why wait to learn about your very own state? It's an exciting place and reading about it now will give you a head start for that time when you "officially" study our state history! Enjoy,

Carole Marsh

California
Let's Have Words!

Make as many words as you can from the letters in the words

THE GOLDEN STATE

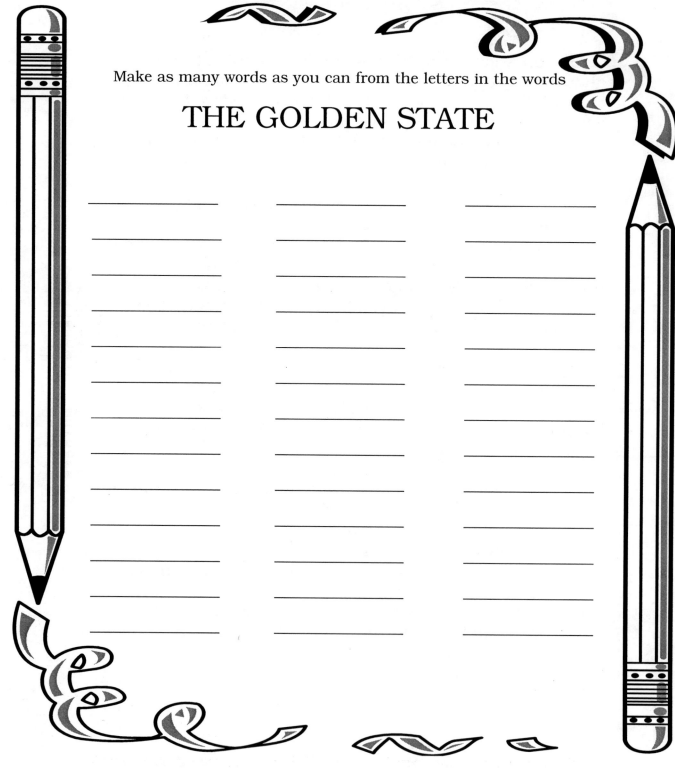

California
The 31st State

Do you know when California became a state? California became the 31st state on September 9, 1850.

Color California red. Color the Atlantic and the Pacific Ocean blue. Color the rest of the U.S. states shown here green.

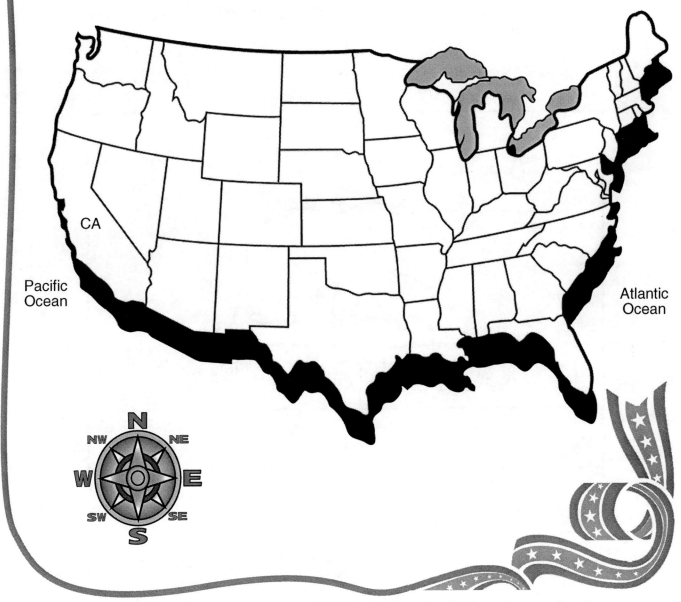

California
State Flag

Do you feel proud when you see the California state flag flying overhead? California's state flag was adopted in 1911. The flag shows a white field with a grizzly bear standing on a patch of green grass above the words "California Republic"; there is a red star in the left hand corner and a red stripe at the bottom.

Color the California flag below.

Don't tread on me!

California
State Bird

Most states have a state bird. It reminds us that we should "fly high" to achieve our goals. The California state bird is the California valley quail.

The California valley quail is a bird that lives mainly in the brush and grassy areas of the valley and mountain areas of California. These birds are not desert birds.

Circle your state bird, then color all the birds.

The early bird gets the worm!

FINCH

MOCKINGBIRD

ROBIN

CALIFORNIA VALLEY QUAIL

EAGLE

CARDINAL

California
State Seal and Motto

The California state seal depicts a seated Minerva, the Roman goddess of wisdom, holding a lance as she gazes across the Pacific Ocean. In the sky above the goddess is the state motto, *Eureka,* Greek for "I have found it."

In 25 words or less, explain what this means:

_____

_____

_____

_____

Color the state seal.

Look what I found!

California
State Flower

Every state has a favorite flower. The California state flower is the golden poppy.

Although California's various climates support many plants and flowers, the poppy is found only in the valley and on the mountain slopes of California.

Color the picture of our state flower.

California
State Tree

Our state tree reminds us that our roots should run deep if we want to grow straight and tall! The state tree for California is the California redwood. It is the tallest tree in the world. The redwood is an evergreen tree that can grow as tall as 380 feet tall. Redwoods are native to Northern California and Oregon.

Finish drawing the redwood tree, then color it.

California
State Zoos

In 1936, The San Francisco Zoo exhibited the first panda seen in the United States. The world-famous San Diego Zoo's World Herd helped save the world's rarest antelope, the Arabian oryx.

Match the name of the zoo animal with its picture

ZEBRA

GIRAFFE

MONKEY

BEAR

TIGER

California
State Explorers

Juan Rodríguez Cabrillo dropped anchor at San Diego Bay in 1542. Sir Frances Drake landed just north of San Francisco Bay in 1579 and claimed the land for England. In 1769, Jesuit priest Junípero Serra founded his first mission in San Diego.

Color the things an explorer might have used.

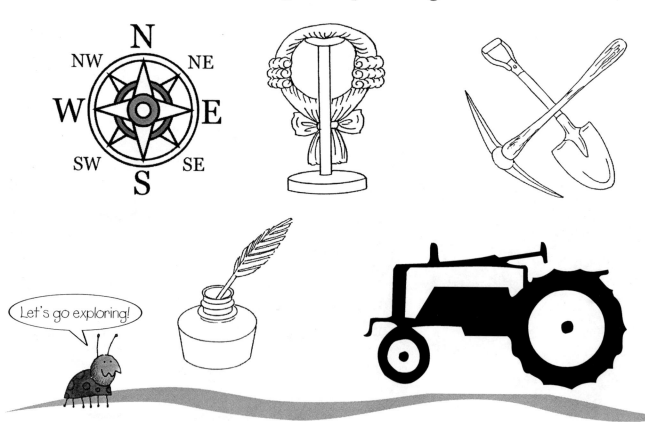

Latin, eh?

California
Dog-face Butterfly
Colias cesonia

The California dog-face butterfly gets its name from two spots on its wings which look like the eyes of a dog.

The California dog-face butterfly has a wingspan about 2 inches (5 centimeters) wide.

Put an X by the insects that are <u>not</u> a California dog-face butterfly and then color all the critters!

California

One Day I Can Vote!

When you are 18 and register according to state laws - you can vote! So please do! Your vote counts!

You are running for a class office.

You get 41 votes!

Here is your opponent!

He gets 16 votes!

ANSWER THE FOLLOWING QUESTIONS:

1. Who won?　　　❏ you　　❏ your opponent

2. How many votes were cast altogether?

3. How many votes did the winner win by?

California
State Capital

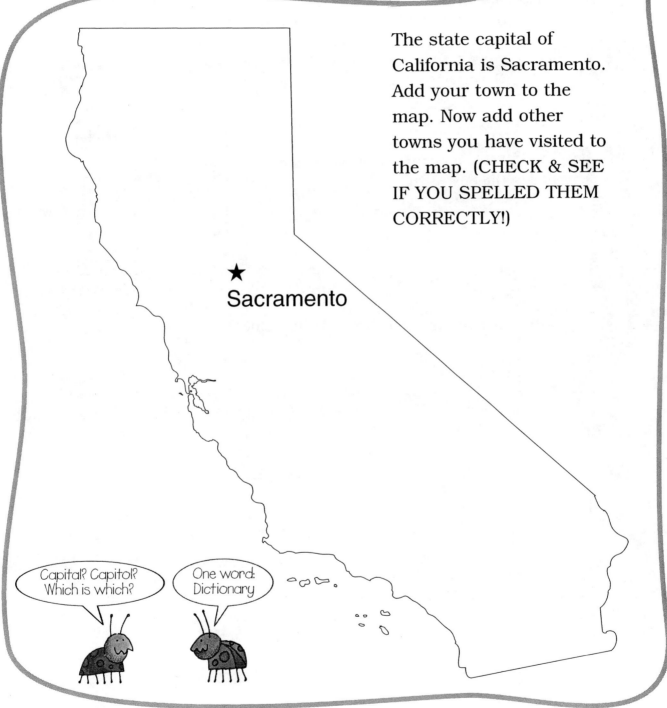

The state capital of California is Sacramento. Add your town to the map. Now add other towns you have visited to the map. (CHECK & SEE IF YOU SPELLED THEM CORRECTLY!)

★
Sacramento

Capital? Capitol? Which is which?

One word: Dictionary

California
Governor

The governor of California is our state's leader.
Do some research to complete the biography of our governor.

Governor's name:
_____

Paste a picture of the governor in
the box.

The governor was born in this state:
_____

The governor has been in office since:
_____

Names of the governor's family members:
_____
_____
_____

Interesting facts about the governor:
_____
_____
_____
_____
_____
_____

California
Crops

Some families in our state make their living from the land.

Some of our state's crops or agricultural products are:

WORD BANK

| corn | grapes | wheat |
| soybeans | beef cattle | peaches |

UNSCRAMBLE THESE IMPORTANT STATE CROPS.

ahtwe _____

rnco _____

sgpare _____

ysnabose _____

febe tlaclte _____

ahepcse _____

California
State Holidays

These are just some of the holidays that California celebrates. Number these holidays in order from the beginning of the year.

Columbus Day 2nd Monday in October	Thanksgiving 4th Thursday in November	Presidents' Day 3rd Monday in February
7	8	2
Independence July 4	California Poppy Day April 6	New Year's Day January 1
5	3	1
Memorial Day last Monday in May	California Admission Day September 9	Christmas December 25
4	6	9

California
Nickname

California has several nicknames. It is called the Golden State, the Eldorado State, and the Grape State.

What other nicknames would suit our state and why?

_____

_____

_____

_____

_____

What nicknames would suit your town or your school?

_____

_____

_____

_____

_____

_____

What's your nickname?

Nick.

California
How BIG is Our State?

Our state is the 3rd largest in the U.S. It is made up of 158,693 square miles.

Can you answer the following questions?

1. How many states are there in the United States?

   _____

2. This many states are smaller than our state:

   _____

3. This many states are larger than our state:

   _____

4. One mile = 5,280 _____ _____ _____ _____

   HINT:

5. Draw a picture of a "square" mile below:

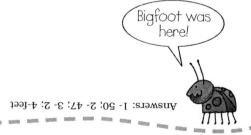

Bigfoot was here!

Answers: 1- 50; 2- 47; 3- 2; 4- feet

California
People

A state is not just towns and mountains and rivers. A state is its people! But the really important people in a state are not famous. You may know them—they may be your mom, your dad, or your teacher. The average, everyday person is the one who makes the state a good state. How? By working hard, by paying taxes, by voting, and by helping California children grow up to be good state citizens!

Match each California person with their accomplishment.

1. Shirley Temple
2. Clint Eastwood
3. Ronald Reagan
4. Greg Louganis
5. Jackie Robinson
6. Kristi Yamaguchi
7. Levi Strauss
8. Jack London
9. John Steinbeck
10. Maya Angelou
11. William Randolph Hearst
12. Luis Alvarez

A. author of *The Grapes of Wrath*
B. first African American to play major league baseball
C. child actress
D. inventor of blue jeans
E. publisher
F. four time Olympic gold medalist for diving
G. actor, director, Oscar winner
H. poet and San Francisco street car conductor
I. figure skating gold-medalist
J. actor, fortieth U.S. president
K. wrote *Call of the Wild*
L. physicist, educator

Answers: 1-C; 2-G; 3-J; 4-F; 5-B; 6-I; 7-D; 8-K; 9-A; 10-H; 11-E; 12-L;

California
Gazetteer

A gazetteer is a list of places. Use the word bank to complete the names of some of these famous places in our state:

1. LOS _ _ _ _ _ _ _

2. SAN _ _ _ _ _ _ _ _ _

3. THE _ _ _ _ _ _ _ GATE BRIDGE

4. _ _ _ _ _ _ _ _ _ _ STUDIOS

5. KNOTTS _ _ _ _ _ FARM

6. NAPA _ _ _ _ _ _ _

7. LA _ _ _ _ TAR PITTS

8. SIERRA _ _ _ _ _ _ _

9. _ _ _ _ _ _ _ DESERT

10. _ _ _ _ _ _ _ TREE

WORD BANK

Los Angeles   Napa Valley
San Francisco   La Brea Tar Pitts
Golden Gate Bridge   Sierra Nevada
Universal Studios   Mojave Desert
Knotts Berry Farm   Joshua Tree

California
Neighbors

No person or state lives alone. You have neighbors where you live. Sometimes they may be right next door. Other times, they may be way down the road. But you live in the same neighborhood and are interested in what goes on there.

You have neighbors at school. The children who sit in front, beside, or behind you are your neighbors. You may share books. You might borrow a pencil. They might ask you to move so they can see the board better.

We have a lot in common with our state neighbors. Some of our land is alike. We share some history. We care about our part of the country. We share borders. Some of our people go there; some of their people come here. Most of the time we get along with our state neighbors. Even when we argue or disagree, it is a good idea for both of us to work it out. After all, states are not like people—they can't move away!

Use the color key to color California and its neighbors.

Color Key:

California–red
Arizona–yellow
Mexico–purple
Pacific Ocean–blue
Oregon–orange
Nevada–green

California
Highs and Lows

The highest point in the state is Mount Whitney. Mount Whitney is 14,494 feet (4,417 meters) above sea level.

Draw a picture of Mount Whitney.

The lowest point in the state is Death Valley. Death Valley is in the Mojave Desert. Death Valley is 282 feet (86 meters) below sea level.

Draw a picture of Death Valley.

California
Old Man River

California has many great rivers. Rivers give us water for our crops. Rivers are also water "highways." On these water highways travel crops, manufactured goods, people, and many other things—including children in tire tubes!

Here are some of California's most important rivers:

> The Sacramento River
> The San Joaquin River
> The Colorado River

Draw a kid "tubing" down a California River!

California
Weather ... Or Not!

What kind of climate does our state have?
- Cold in the mountains
- Dry and breezy in the south
- Dry and hot in the desert
- The average winter temperature is about 44°F (7°C).
- The average summer temperature is about 75°F (24°C).

You might think adults talk about the weather a lot. But our state's weather is very important to us. Crops need water and sunshine. Weather can affect the tourist industry. Good weather can mean more money for our state. Bad weather can cause problems that cost money.

ACTIVITY: Do you watch the nightly news at your house? If you do, you might see the weather report. Tonight, tune in the weather report. The reporter often talks about our state's regions, cities and towns, and our neighboring states. Watching the weather report is a great way to learn about our state. It also helps you know what to wear to school tomorrow!

What is the weather outside now? Draw a picture.

California
Indian Tribes

The American Indians were first on our land, long before it was a state.

California's main Indian tribes:

HOOPA   PAIUTE   YUROK
KAROK   MODOC   YAHI   CHEROKEE

Help Maize find her way through the maize (corn) field maze to her hut made of saplings!

Start

Finish

California
Website Page

Here is a website you can go to and learn more about California:
www.state.ca.us

Design your own state website page on the computer screen below.

Can you dig Archaeology?

Our state's fossil is the saber tooth tiger.

California

State Song

Here is the first verse of our state song:

TITLE: *I Love You California*

VERSE 1:
    I love you, California, you're the greatest state of all;
    I love you in the winter, summer, spring and fall;
    I love your fertile valleys; your dear mountains I adore;
    I love your grand old ocean and I love her rugged shore.

NOW, WRITE A SECOND VERSE!

_____

_____

_____

_____

_____

_____

_____

_____

_____

_____

_____

California
Spelling Bee!

What's All The Buzz About?

Here are some words related to your state. See if you can find them in the Word Search below.

WORD LIST

STATE	RIVER	PEOPLE	TREE	BIRD
FLAG	VOTE	FLOWER	SONG	OCEAN

```
A  X  N  Y  H  N  V  S  D  G  T  R  E  P
V  O  T  E  M  A  C  S  E  A  B  A  Y  E
S  N  B  R  X  B  R  K  S  X  B  D  S  O
Y  B  P  Q  L  S  O  N  G  R  I  J  H  P
R  I  V  E  R  P  P  L  R  T  Y  U  E  L
Q  R  E  R  T  Y  Z  E  E  R  T  O  N  E
R  D  P  P  A  H  A  O  N  E  C  K  A  R
S  X  O  C  E  A  N  C  P  W  E  R  N  I
P  O  B  U  Y  U  Y  H  E  O  L  L  D  O
Q  U  F  L  A  G  R  K  R  L  X  Z  O  P
Z  X  R  D  G  H  R  E  U  F  L  L  A  L
M  R  D  W  Q  N  M  N  S  T  A  T  E  Z
```

California
Trivia

I ♥ California!

Indians were the first people in California. They lived here over 15,000 years ago.

English, Russian, and Spanish explorers came to California about 300 years ago.

Mexico ceded California to the United States in 1848.

The California Gold Rush began in 1849.

California became the 31st state in 1850.

San Francisco's great earthquake killed 700 people in 1906.

The first commercial film, *The Count of Monte Cristo*, was made in Los Angeles in 1908.

The Golden Gate Bridge was completed in 1937.

Many Californians fought during World War II. Those left at home worked to supply food and other goods for the war. Some were held in internment camps. Californians also fought in the Vietnam War and the Gulf War.

California's state colors are blue and gold.

The United Nations was founded in San Francisco in 1945.

President Richard Nixon, a California native, is the only president who ever resigned from office.

The Hollywood Chamber of Commerce cleans the Hollywood Walk of Fame every single day!